Saints of Africa

by
Jean Olwen Maynard

*All booklets are published thanks to the
generous support of the members of the
Catholic Truth Society*

CATHOLIC TRUTH SOCIETY
PUBLISHERS TO THE HOLY SEE

Contents

Images: Page 28, detail from *The 22 Martyrs of Uganda* by Albert Wider (1962). By kind permission of The Josephite House of Studies, New Orleans, USA. Other images: every effort has been made to trace the copyright holders. The publisher would be grateful to receive any further information.

All rights reserved. First published 2015 by The Incorporated Catholic Truth Society, 40-46 Harleyford Road London SE11 5AY Tel: 020 7640 0042 Fax: 020 7640 0046. © 2015 The Incorporated Catholic Truth Society.

ISBN 978 1 78469 037 3

Christianity in Africa

The Gospel of Jesus Christ began to be proclaimed in Africa at a very early date, but eighteen centuries were to pass before it made any significant impact on the sub-Saharan region. Why was this? There's no easy answer, but we know that God is the lord of history, and even when we can't fully understand the how or the why, it's important to know something of the course of events.

North Africa was an integral part of the Roman-ruled Mediterranean, and its two most important ports - Alexandria, on the Nile Delta, and Carthage (in modern Tunisia) - undoubtedly became centres of Christian activity from the first century AD. Alexandria was already an established powerhouse of Greek learning, and by the second century its catechetical school was making a distinctive contribution to the development of Christian theology: it produced St Clement of Alexandria and Origen. Meanwhile, a vibrant Christianity developed in Rome's African provinces westwards of Egypt, where the towns were thoroughly latinised in language and culture. It was there, rather than in Italy, that the production of Christian literature in Latin began. A great many African Christians gave their lives for their faith during the Roman persecutions, including St Perpetua and St Felicity who are among the most famous martyr-saints of the early Church. The first Latin-speaking Bishop of Rome was St Victor, who hailed from Carthage, and the first Latin theological works came from the pen of the Carthaginian Tertullian. Another influential theologian was St Cyprian, Bishop of Carthage for ten years up to his martyrdom in 258.

The translation of the Bible into Coptic enabled Christianity to put down deep roots among the peasant farmers of rural Egypt, and it was from among them that St Antony of the Desert, and other pioneers of the worldwide monastic movement, emerged. From Egypt the faith spread to Nubia and Ethiopia, and in 340 St Athanasius, the celebrated Patriarch of Alexandria who so valiantly defended the Nicene Creed against the Arians (who refused to accept that the Son is consubstantial with the Father), consecrated the first bishop for Ethiopia. Later in the fourth century the persistent prayers of St Monica, a housewife from Tagaste (in Algeria), obtained the conversion of her wayward son Augustine. He went on to become bishop of the coastal town of Hippo (in Tunisia), and one of the greatest theologians of all time. In 431 another Patriarch of Alexandria, St Cyril, convened the Council of Ephesus which upheld the tradition of honouring Our Lady as Mother of God. As with other early Church Councils, the issue at stake was essentially what we should believe about the Divinity of Christ and about the Holy Trinity, and the same was true of the Council of Chalcedon in 451. However, large sections of the Church rejected Chalcedon. Modern theologians think the dispute may have been essentially a misunderstanding, and that the two sides are not really all that far apart in their beliefs. But feelings at the time ran strong, leading to a major split which remains unhealed to this day. In Egypt the split followed cultural lines: the Greek-speakers accepted Chalcedon, but the Copts did not.

Arrival of Islam

Muslim forces swept out of Arabia in the seventh century, conquered the Middle East and Egypt with astonishing rapidity, then proceeded steadily westwards to secure the rest of North Africa. The Christian inhabitants were classed as inferior to Muslims and subjected to a special tax, but were not forced to convert. Large numbers are known to have preserved their faith by migrating to Italy, but as the years passed those who remained began to convert to Islam. Between apostasy and emigration the Christian communities underwent a slow but steady attrition, and the last communication between the Pope and the Bishop of Carthage - the sole bishop then remaining - was in 1076.

In Egypt the Copts struggled to hold out against a constant grinding pressure of discriminatory treatment, punctuated by occasional outbursts of violent persecution: though reduced to a small minority, they did not disappear.

Nubia was overrun and largely Islamised in the fourteenth century, but Ethiopia, though hemmed in on all sides, preserved its independence as a Christian kingdom. The Egyptian patriarchs, based now in Cairo, continued to provide bishops, but would only send one at a time. When he died, the Ethiopians had to put together an expedition to make the difficult journey to Cairo to fetch a successor. The Coptic Church regarded all Chalcedonian Christians as heretics, so naturally refused to recognise any of the later saints venerated by the Catholic Church, instead canonising hundreds of Coptic saints.

The lands of Islam formed a barrier severing Europe from Asia and Africa, until in the fifteenth century the Portuguese learned how to navigate round the westward "bulge" of the African continent. They established a vast seaborne empire across Africa and Asia, controlled through a network of fortified coastal bases and alliances with local rulers. The Pope granted them a monopoly on the promotion of Catholic missions in the region, and numerous priests were sent out, despite the fearful death toll from tropical infections to which Europeans had no immunity. Over the next few centuries small Christian communities were formed in many parts of Africa, either around a nucleus of Portuguese settlers and their mixed-race families, or else around the courts of friendly and receptive African rulers. Yet their overall numbers were low, and their impact negligible. The Portuguese did provide vital support to Ethiopia: Africa's sole surviving Christian kingdom would have been extinguished in 1543 by a Muslim invasion, had it not been for their military assistance. However, a subsequent attempt by the Jesuits to impose Roman Catholicism got them thrown out.

Missionary Activity

Newly emerging Protestant maritime powers established bases of their own on the African coast. However, they rarely showed any interest in mission to non-Christians. Meanwhile, Islam was achieving large numbers of conversions, and any well-informed observer taking stock in the early decades of the nineteenth century would have confidently predicted that Africa was destined to become an all-Muslim continent. Nevertheless, those same decades saw an unprecedented awakening of missionary enthusiasm among both Catholics and Protestants.

The missionaries saw themselves as ambassadors of God, but they could not help also being seen as emissaries of their home countries - particularly of Britain and France, where most missionary societies had their headquarters. African rulers often saw them as potential political assets, if only as a channel of access to advanced technology which could enhance their power and prestige. Both missionaries and indigenous Christians could also be perceived as a political threat - stalking horses for the annexing of Africa by Europe, which in due course came to pass. Up to 1880, however, the European powers were interested more in acquiring strategic bases and spheres of influence, and access to raw materials, than extensive territorial possessions in the African interior. Meanwhile, the most significant imperial aggrandisement project in north-eastern Africa was indigenous: Egypt was carving out a huge colony in what would become Sudan, and threatening to encroach on all the neighbouring territories.

A point which cannot be sufficiently stressed is that white missionaries never made more than a few converts. Christianity only "took off" in Africa when Africans began evangelising Africans.

Blessed Ghebre-Michael

Ghebre-Michael (the name means "servant of St Michael") was born in 1791 in Dibo, a village in west-central Ethiopia, and went to school at the nearby Monastery of Mertule-Mariam ("Tabernacle of Mary"). None of the classes had desks or blackboards, or even a classroom: the students assembled around their teacher in any place that was convenient - the church porch, or under some trees. Books or writing materials, when needed, were balanced on their knees, but a great deal of the learning was done orally, by repetition and memorising. In this way Ghebre-Michael continued his studies until, at the age of twenty-six, he was consecrated as a monk. Illiteracy levels in Ethiopia were very high, even among monks, and a learned monk was a rarity, while books were so scarce that Mertule-Mariam didn't even possess the *Book of the Monks*, which was the basic monastic rule. Ghebre-Michael requested permission to travel around visiting other monasteries to try to find a copy. The other monks gave him their blessing to do so. He spent the next ten years wandering from monastery to monastery, poring over ancient manuscripts, and becoming expert in every branch of ecclesiastical lore.

Blessed Ghebre-Michael

The Ethiopian Church was bitterly divided by theological disputes about Christology. The arguments were tangled and difficult to make sense of, but many of the monks seemed to think that Jesus Christ being God meant he couldn't really be human at the same time. Others appeared to take the view that Jesus was born and lived as a human being up to his baptism, and was then adopted as God's Son. A lot of what he was hearing struck Ghebre-Michael as bizarre and obviously wrong. Certainly it did not fit with what he read in the Scriptures or the early Church Fathers.

His erudition, and his burning passion for truth, attracted a small band of eager students who travelled around and studied with him. Eventually, around 1825, they arrived in Gondar, the seat of both the bishop (when there was one) and the *echage*, a senior abbot who was the recognised spokesman for all the monasteries in Ethiopia. There Ghebre-Michael at last found the *Book of the Monks*. The rich opportunities for theological research and discussion in that city full of churches, monasteries and learned ecclesiastics occupied him for many happy years. However, in 1838 he closed his school. Hungry for a deeper understanding of God, he'd resolved to make a pilgrimage to Jerusalem. This meant heading northwards through Tigre towards the port of Massawa. He took his time, visiting the various monasteries of north-east Ethiopia along the way, and when at last he reached Massawa, he was strongly advised not to risk pursuing his journey alone.

An unexpected travelling companion

Effective central government had long broken down, and the country was divided between regional princes, each ruling his own area as a personal fiefdom. Wubie, Governor of Tigre, was one of the most astute and successful of these local rulers. He had made it his policy to welcome and protect European missionaries and explorers, and hoped to obtain British or French support against the growing threat posed by Egypt. Wubie was about to send an official delegation to Cairo, to ask the Coptic Pope to provide a new bishop for Ethiopia (the last one having died twelve years previously). He warmly welcomed Ghebre-Michael's request to be one of the delegates. Setting off with the rest of the party in January 1841, Ghebre-Michael learned to his disgust that a Vincentian priest named Justin de Jacobis would be travelling with them. This had been insisted on by Wubie, who knew that the presence of a European would deter potential attackers. The journey involved sailing for two and a half months up the Red Sea in a small Arab ship, followed by a four-day trek across the desert to Cairo. Thus, the delegates had plenty of time to get to know Fr Justin quite well. They found him to be completely different from their stereotypical image of a Roman Catholic missionary. He was humble and helpful; moreover, he'd happily adopted the Ethiopian lifestyle, wore Ethiopian clothes and showed the utmost respect for the Ethiopian spiritual tradition. Despite himself, Ghebre-Michael couldn't help liking Fr Justin.

By contrast, his initial audiences with the Coptic Pope in Cairo left him quite upset. Pope Boutros VII agreed to provide a new bishop, but the delegation was astonished when he presented Andreas, a monk aged only twenty-one. Andreas had benefited from a western education, having attended an Anglican missionary school, but his grasp of theology seemed very limited. Ghebre-Michael vehemently opposed the Pope's choice, which infuriated Andreas: he abused the venerable monk, calling him a nasty half-blind old man. Ghebre-Michael, who'd lost an eye in childhood, replied calmly that it hadn't affected his understanding of the holy mysteries. Nevertheless the rest of the delegation reluctantly gave way, and Andreas was duly consecrated. On becoming a bishop he took a new name as well as a new title: from then on he would be known as Abuna Salama. The delegation did not return home immediately, as Fr Justin took them first to Rome to meet Pope Gregory XVI, and then to the Holy Land where they stayed for three months. They eventually returned to Cairo to find that Abuna Salama had set off for Ethiopia without them, the Anglicans having arranged for him to travel under official British protection. In his absence Ghebre-Michael had another audience with Pope Boutros, and this one went much better than before. He was assured that the Coptic Church believed, and had always believed, that Jesus Christ is both true God and true Man, and he was given a letter to this effect to deliver to Abuna Salama.

Still accompanied by Fr Justin, the delegation arrived back at Massawa in April 1842. Ghebre-Michael made his way to Gondar, where he persuaded the *echage* and other church leaders to assemble a synod to consider the letter he'd brought from Pope Boutros. Abuna Salama arranged for the synod to meet at his house. When it was ready to start he asked for the letter, and Ghebre-Michael trustingly handed it over, but he simply put it straight into his pocket. A public showdown followed. Abuna Salama declared Ghebre-Michael excommunicated as a rebel against his bishop. Ghebre-Michael retorted that Abuna Salama was himself in rebellion against Pope Boutros, and therefore had no authority to excommunicate.

Ethiopian and Catholic

Ghebre-Michael spent the next five months in prayer and reflection, seeking God's guidance. In September 1843 he travelled to Tigre, found Fr Justin and asked to become a Catholic. Rather than immediately agreeing, Fr Justin suggested taking a little more time for theological research, and for the next few months happily accompanied him on his travels around the monastic libraries. His resolution confirmed, in February 1844 Ghebre-Michael was received into communion with the Catholic Church.

Small but significant numbers of other Ethiopians, including monks and priests, and even some parishes, reached similar decisions around this time. Thus came about the foundation of an Ethiopian Catholic Church, thoroughly Ethiopian in liturgy, culture and spirituality, as envisioned by Fr Justin. Meanwhile, Abuna Salama was finding it impossible to establish any effective episcopal authority. He was at odds with the *echage*, and none of the princes would support him. In 1845 Ras Ali, the ruler of Gondar, exiled him to Tigre where he spent many years seething with frustration at his powerlessness. He did what he could to harass the Catholic mission, but he could not destroy it.

An upstart warlord named Kassa launched a remarkably successful campaign to fight his way to the top, and in June 1853 defeated Ras Ali in pitched battle. Deeply devout, Kassa was fired with the vision of reuniting Ethiopia as a proud and independent nation under himself as king, and of reuniting and reviving its national church. He immediately recalled Abuna Salama from exile. The Catholic leaders waited in Gondar, in trepidation, as the Coptic bishop journeyed in triumph towards the city. Though they were urged to flee, Fr Justin decided he couldn't abandon his flock and everything he'd built up: he hoped to talk Kassa round. He advised everyone else to escape, but Ghebre-Michael declared: "I have very bad feet and rheumatism. I prefer to die here for the faith than to die of sickness on the road." The others also refused to leave, and soon it was too late.

Arrest and imprisonment

In July 1854, shortly after making his triumphant entry into Gondar, Kassa decreed that everyone must accept Abuna Salama's definitions of Christian doctrine, or "be shortened top and bottom" (meaning they'd have first their feet cut off and then be beheaded). Some of the braver Ethiopian churchmen nevertheless sought to question the youthful bishop's definitions, which appeared to deny Christ's humanity, but he refused any discussion: "First accept my faith, and then I will instruct you…"

The Catholics were all arrested. Fr Justin was imprisoned separately, to await deportation, but the Ethiopians were handed over to Abuna Salama who was determined to break them. Ghebre-Michael and four others were subjected to the torture of the *ghend*: their legs were put through a hole in a heavy log and squeezed tightly with wooden pegs hammered in, and they were left there, with just enough food and water to keep them alive for five months. In December they were released from the *ghend* and brought before an ecclesiastical tribunal, but the tribunal refused to impose the death penalty over a question of doctrine. Frustrated, the bishop had Ghebre-Michael flogged, then handed him over to Kassa. Kassa threatened to have him executed. Ghebre-Michael told him to go ahead.

For the next few months Kassa had more important things to worry about, because Wubie was advancing to meet him with a large army. The battle took place on 9th February 1855, and Kassa was victorious. Two days later he was crowned by Abuna Salama, and changed his name to Tewodros (Theodore) in line with a prophecy that a King Theodore would one day arise and bring in an era of peace and happiness.

Ghebre-Michael remained impervious to threats and ill-treatment. When Tewodros set off on a new campaign against the ruler of the southern province of Shewa, he ordered the prisoner brought along. In late May the British Consul, Walter Plowden, joined the Emperor at his encampment. Tewodros summoned the recalcitrant monk before him one last time, in Plowden's presence, and demanded his submission. Ghebre-Michael replied: "You have authority over my body, but over my soul you have no authority. Moreover, it is against all justice for any human power to declare: 'I will kill you if you do not embrace my belief.'" The Emperor ordered him taken away and shot, but Plowden intervened. Instead, therefore, Ghebre-Michael was condemned to march behind the army in heavy chains for the rest of his life. The soldiers detailed to guard him did their best to alleviate his sufferings, until on 29th August he told them the end was near, and they laid him down in the shadow of a tree, resting against a large stone. Calm and serene, he foretold the disasters that would shortly befall Tewodros and Ethiopia, and then quietly died. He was beatified in 1926.

Blessed Ghebre-Michael, you were brought to recognise and embrace in all its fulness the mystery of Jesus Christ, true God and true Man, and to lay down your life for conscience's sake. By your example and intercession, keep us always faithful to the teachings of the Church. Through Christ our Lord. Amen.

St Josephine Bakhita

In approximately 1876 a little girl gathering herbs near her home in Darfur, in Sudan, was brutally abducted by two strangers. Threatening her with a knife and a gun, the two men forced her to go with them, walking non-stop for the rest of the day and all through the night. She was about to collapse with exhaustion when they reached the men's village, where they locked her up in a storeroom and left her to cry herself to sleep. They'd told her her name was now Bakhita, meaning "Lucky." She soon forgot her real name. She was no older than eight or nine.

The traumatised child was kept locked up for a month, then sold to a slave merchant who marched her off with his other captives. The adult men and women were chained together, while Bakhita and another little girl walked together at the back, unfettered but under the eyes of the merchant and his men. Each day they were driven further from their home area until, after a journey of several weeks, they arrived at El Obeid.

Sold and abused

Bakhita became house-slave to a wealthy family. At first it wasn't too bad: the master's daughters treated her as a kind of pet. But one day she did something that annoyed their

St Josephine Bakhita

brother, and he flew into a temper and beat her, kicking her
unconscious. When she recovered she was sold to a general
in the Egyptian army which was occupying Sudan. The
occupation had led to a major escalation of the slave trade
in the region, and although the Egyptian government had
ordered its suppression, the general's behaviour showed
how seriously such decrees were taken by its agents in
the field. Bakhita's duties required her to be constantly
attending to the general's wife and mother - dressing and
perfuming them, fanning them and running their errands.
She never minded the work as such, but they were cruel
mistresses. All the slaves were worked from early morning
until late into the night, and constantly hit and beaten for
the slightest mistake. On one occasion when the general
had a row with his wife, he took it out on Bakhita and
another slave-girl, though it was nothing to do with them:
he dragged them into the yard and made them lie on the
ground, face up, while two of his soldiers administered a
brutal caning across their upper legs. On another occasion
Bakhita was forced to submit to a painful tattooing process:
cuts were made in her skin in a decorative pattern, all over
the front of her body and along her right arm, and salt
rubbed in. She spent the next three months on her sleeping
mat, unable to move for the pain.

Following the revolt sparked in Sudan in 1881 by the
self-proclaimed Mahdi, Bakhita's master decided to get
out, and began selling off his slaves. A few, including

Bakhita, were selected to be taken and sold in Khartoum, and there Bakhita was purchased by the Italian consular agent Calisto Legnani. Slaves were plentiful and cheap in Sudan, and even Europeans didn't see anything wrong in keeping a few to make their lifestyle more comfortable. Legnani treated his slaves well, and Bakhita was very happy, and devoted to her new master. Up to the very end of 1884, when Khartoum was under siege by the Mahdists, she knew nothing of the deepening crisis. But when Legnani mentioned that he was planning to go to Italy, something impelled her to ask that he take her with him. Amused by her request, he agreed. A month later the city fell, but by then Legnani and Bakhita, together with a friend of Legnani named Augusto Michieli, had reached Suakin on the Red Sea Coast. Thanks to the Suez Canal, and the steamship companies that ran regular passenger services, getting from there to Genoa was safe, easy and quick.

The Catechumenate in Venice

Augusto's wife, Maria Turina, came to meet him in Genoa, and as soon as she saw Bakhita, said she needed a nursemaid. Legnani casually gave the girl to her as a present, and the Michielis took her to live in Mirano, near Venice, to take care of their baby daughter Mimmina. But Augusto was anxious to return to his old stomping grounds in Africa. Once he'd sized up how things were going, and that the Madhists were unlikely to attack Suakin, he returned to open a hotel. The whole family went out for an extended visit, and it was all planned that Bakhita would be part of the enterprise, serving behind the bar. In the autumn of 1887 Maria Turina returned to Mirano, accompanied by Bakhita and the baby, to set about selling the house before they all moved permanently to Suakin.

The house sale was prolonged and complex, requiring frequent visits from the Michielis' local agent Illuminato Checchini. Checchini was shocked to discover that Bakhita had never received any religious instruction. The Michielis were not religious people, and it had never occurred to them. Towards the end of 1888, when Maria Turina was planning a trip to Suakin to see her husband, Checchini arranged for Bakhita and Mimmina to stay at the Catechumenate in Venice. This was a venerable institution originally intended for adult non-Christians who wished to convert to Christianity - though Checchini omitted to explain that to Maria Turina. For one year Bakhita was looked after by the Canossian Sisters at the Catechumenate, and instructed in the Christian faith. When Maria Turina at last came to fetch her, she refused to go.

Maria Turina stormed and raged. The Sisters were embarrassed and tried to persuade Bakhita to do as she was asked. The situation tore Bakhita apart: she was genuinely fond of the Michieli family, and grateful for all they'd done for her. Nevertheless, she held firm. The Patriarch of Venice was brought into the argument, and he in turn sought guidance from the Italian government. The ruling came back that slavery did not exist in Italy; therefore Bakhita was a free woman, and could not be compelled to return to Africa. Little Mimmina clung to Bakhita, begging her to come, but Maria Turina grabbed the child and stormed out. Bakhita was left weeping bitterly, but she knew she'd done the right thing.

She was baptised on 9th January 1890, and given the baptismal name Josephine in honour of a sponsor from the Venetian nobility. The Patriarch confirmed her and gave her First Communion. Up to then, she'd always seemed to have a sadness inside her, which was only natural in view of all that she had suffered, but the sadness now disappeared and she seemed transfigured with joy. She was only supposed to stay at the Catechumenate for one year after her baptism, but the Sisters kindly allowed her to stay for nearly four, and by then she'd become convinced that God was calling her to become a Sister herself. She began her novitiate in December 1893, and was professed in December 1896.

Mother Josephine

From then on she was known officially as Mother Josephine. She never returned to Africa. In 1902 she was transferred to the Canossian House in Schio, where she spent the rest of her life (which was, for the most part, peaceful and happy). Initially, she worked in the convent kitchen, and in 1907 she was promoted to be head cook.

During the First World War, when the convent became a temporary field hospital, she helped to nurse wounded soldiers. Afterwards she served for many years as portress, dealing with everyone who called at the convent. Increasingly people began going there just to talk to her, to pour out their worries and seek her advice.

In 1930, in obedience to her Superior General, she recounted her life story to be written for publication, and it became a best-seller. For several years after that she was assigned to travel around with another nun to promote, and help raise funds for, the congregation's overseas missions. Her companion, an experienced missionary, did most of the talking and explained Bakhita's story on her behalf: at the end she'd just ask Mother Josephine to say a few words, whereupon Bakhita would hop up, thank everyone for coming and say simply, "Be good. Love Our Lord." Sometimes she added, "Pray for those who don't yet know him. It's such a great grace to know God!" Then she sat down again.

Telling her story

Her public appearances proved wildly popular with Italian audiences, with queues to see her often causing traffic jams for miles around. But although she cared deeply about building support for the missions, she hated the public appearances. In Schio she could relate to people as people, but being the focus of intense curiosity from a large crowd of complete strangers was disturbing, and she particularly disliked the way, listening to her story, they all felt sorry for her and kept saying, "Poor thing, poor thing." There was no way she could explain to them how she felt, but to her fellow Sisters she was very clear: "I'm not a poor thing because I belong to the Master, and I'm in his house. People who don't know Our Lord - they're the ones who are poor!" Knowing herself enfolded in God's love had brought full healing of the trauma of her early life. "If I were to meet those who kidnapped me," she insisted, "or even those who tortured me, I would kneel down and kiss their hands. Because, if those things had not happened, I would not have become a Christian and would not be a Sister today."

During the Second World War Bakhita assured the people of Schio that none of their houses would be bombed. They were already convinced she was a saint, so they believed her, and all turned out as she'd said. After a long period of illness and infirmity, she died peacefully on 8th February 1947. She was canonised in 2000, and her feast day, 8th February, has been made a day of prayer for victims of human trafficking.

St Josephine Bakhita, you were brought from abject slavery to the dignity of being a daughter of God and bride of Christ. By your example and intercession, help us to find healing for the wounds we have suffered in the past, and to look to the future with joy and trust. Through Christ our Lord, Amen.

The Martyr Saints of Uganda

Kalemba was born in approximately 1836 in Busoga - one of a number of traditional African kingdoms within what would become Uganda. As a child he was captured by raiders and carried off to the neighbouring kingdom of Buganda. There he was placed with a family that treated him more as an adopted son than as a slave. He grew up tall and strong, and became an official in the service of a local chief known as the Mukwenda. Over the years he gained an excellent reputation as a trustworthy aide, an honest judge who never took bribes, and a brave warrior. He also grew quite rich, and was able to marry three wives who worked all day on his farm, growing all the food the family needed, and adding to his wealth. He himself never lifted a finger on the farm: that was women's work, and far beneath the dignity of such an important man.

Traders from the eastern Swahili Coast began travelling to Buganda, bringing guns and gunpowder, plus beads and cotton cloth to exchange for ivory and slaves. All the trading was done with the Kabaka, who was absolute ruler of Buganda and controlled its wealth. From around 1867 a fairly flexible form of Islam became popular at the court of the Kabaka Mutesa I, near Kampala. Mutesa himself led the

The Martyr Saints of Uganda

prayers in the mosque, though neither he, nor most of the courtiers who took up the new fashionable religion, saw any need to abandon their traditional religious practices, or alter their lifestyle. But Kalemba, who felt in his heart a deep longing for God, embraced Islam with deep sincerity. After some years, other Muslims began arriving from Sudan who took a more hard-line approach, and openly disapproved of the uncircumcised Kabaka acting as *imam*. Mutesa then grew increasingly chary of Islam, seeing it as a rival to his own authority. He was very annoyed to realise that some of his courtiers were taking this new religion seriously.

Service at the Kabaka's court could open up fantastic opportunities. Any promising lad might be accepted as a page, and some had started off as slaves, but others were highly-born, and places were eagerly sought after for the sons of the powerful and wealthy. Nevertheless, life in and around the palace was lived on a knife edge: any wrong move could lead to sudden death. One day Mutesa abruptly ordered that all the court Muslims be rounded up and executed: about a hundred were taken to Namugongo - a traditional execution site two days' journey away - and killed there. Kalemba, and the other Muslims who survived, got the message: they learned to keep their heads down.

Exploring Christianity

In 1875 Mutesa received a visit from the British explorer Henry Morton Stanley, who persuaded him to issue an appeal for missionaries. The Kabaka was probably hoping for British support against the threat of an Egyptian invasion, and in fact Britain did intervene to warn Egypt to back off. Meanwhile, in 1877, a small party of Anglican missionaries disembarked at the port of Bagamoyo (in Tanzania) and followed the trail blazed by the Swahili to reach the Kabaka's court. Mutesa showed great interest in what they had to say. He invited them to read aloud passages from the Bible in his presence, and said that Christianity sounded like a better religion than Islam. Kalemba started to think so too. He went to call on the missionaries and asked for instruction.

In 1879 a group of White Fathers arrived. Mutesa summoned the Mukwenda and ordered him to construct a house for them. The task was delegated to Kalemba. The Anglicans warned him to be very careful, telling him that the religion of these Catholics wasn't really Christian, but something quite evil. However Kalemba decided to make up his own mind. The Mukwenda asked to be taught the Catholic faith, and Kalemba attended the instruction sessions with him. As soon as the Fathers explained that Christians were only allowed to have one wife, the Mukwenda lost interest. But Kalemba listened carefully, and arranged to separate from all his wives except one: Kikuvwa.

During his regular visits to the mission, Kalemba got to know two high-flying young courtiers. Kaggwa was originally from Bunyoro, another of the local kingdoms:

like Kalemba he'd been captured in a raid, and because he was good-looking been presented to the Kabaka and made a royal page. When the White Fathers arrived he was around twenty-five years old. He told his friend Mukasa that he'd decided to become a Catholic, and Mukasa said he would do the same. Mukasa had been born into a well-to-do family in Buganda: he'd been a page for about six years, and was now in his early twenties. The prospective catechumens were warned that being a Christian was a serious matter, and they must be prepared to die rather than deny Jesus Christ. They said they understood. Shortly after beginning their instruction, Kaggwa was promoted to be master of the royal drummers, and Mukasa to become Mutesa's personal attendant.

A slave of Christ

The White Fathers were amazed at the eagernesss of Kalemba, Kaggwa and Mukasa. The Fathers had no idea that the trio also used to visit the Anglicans for Bible study, and would probably have been horrified if they'd found out, but they never did. After only two years they decided these three were ready for baptism. The White Fathers followed the common missionary custom of giving a saint's name at baptism, and Kaggwa and Mukasa were given the names Andrew and Joseph. Kalemba, who was given the name Matthias, from then on made further changes in his lifestyle. He often used to help his remaining wife, Kikuvwa, on the farm and with the housework, and when he was travelling he even carried his own luggage, rather than having a slave carry it for him as his rank entitled him to do. The other officials found this strange, but he told them: "Am I not a slave, the slave of Jesus Christ?" Whenever his chief went to war, Kalemba fought as courageously as ever, but he refused to take part in the usual looting and enslavement of women and children.

The Kabaka constantly gave the impression he was on the verge of conversion - but to which religion? Sometimes it was Islam, sometimes Anglicanism, sometimes Catholicism. Meanwhile, he had power of life and death over everyone, his moods were unpredictable, and rumours were constantly flying. In November 1882 the White Fathers came to feel that the level of threat, whether for themselves or for their converts, had just then become unacceptably high. So although the Anglicans saw no reason to leave, the White Fathers withdrew from Buganda, and resettled on the far side of Lake Victoria. They remained away for nearly three years.

In their absence, the Catholic pages and court officials continued to evangelise and give religious instruction. Andrew Kaggwa, and his assistant bandsman Buzabaliawo who was still a catechumen, regularly catechised the crown prince Mwanga, and made sure he said his prayers. During 1884 Buganda was ravaged by an epidemic of bubonic plague, followed by smallpox. Kaggwa and some of the other Christians looked after those who fell sick, baptised the dying, and gave them proper burial. In October Mutesa I died in the arms of Joseph Mukasa. He'd never committed himself to any of the foreign religions, and probably never really intended to, but he did give orders forbidding the hundreds of human sacrifices which were customarily carried out to mark the passing of a Kabaka. Eighteen-year-old Mwanga, who succeeded him, confirmed Mukasa in his post as personal attendant, and also promoted him to be majordomo. Kaggwa was made bandmaster-general, and given a grant of land at Kigowa, where his house quickly became a centre of Christian activity.

"Do not kill that white man"

A number of young men arrived at court to become pages in the service of the new Kabaka, and were kitted out in the uniform which was simple but stylish: a cane necklet, and a piece of white cloth draped over the right shoulder. Some of the newcomers were quite young: there was one boy named Kizito who was only about thirteen. Others were older. Lwanga, who was about the same age as Mukasa, had already learned a great deal about Christianity, not directly from the missionaries but from friends who were Catholic catechumens. Being already adult, and having made a good impression, he was placed over the other pages. Lwanga and Mukasa took charge of giving religious instruction to those who wanted to become Catholics, and when the White Fathers returned in July 1885 they found 800 eager candidates being prepared for baptism in the Catholic Church.

Those who'd accepted Christianity up to then included a high proportion of the royal pages and court officials: some were Catholics and some were Anglicans. The rival groups of missionaries were constantly at loggerheads, but this did not bother their converts. What did worry them was the attitude of the new Kabaka: he was a predatory homosexual with a liking for adolescent boys. He frequently made immoral demands of the younger pages, and Mukasa had to keep telling them that it was their right and duty to say, "No." But anyone who refused the Kabaka whatever he wanted could be killed out of hand.

In September 1885 two pieces of news reached the court. One was that the Germans had occupied Bagamoyo; the other was that an Anglican bishop, James Hannington, was on his way to Buganda, travelling via Busoga. Alarm bells rang in the Kabaka's mind: these Europeans were becoming a serious threat! His perspicacity deserves some credit: the occupation of Bagamoyo was indeed part of the process which historians call the "Scramble for Africa," whereby the European powers suddenly began to slice up Africa like a cake and share it between them. However Bishop Hannington was in no sense the vanguard of a British invasion, and the action the Kabaka determined on was not going to help Buganda. He secretly ordered a band of warriors to intercept the bishop and his companions, and kill them.

Mukasa tried to argue with him to cancel the order: "Do not kill that white man, for if you do, you will have to answer for it before God." Mwanga flew into a rage and ordered Mukasa out of his sight; he went to his hut and spent the whole night in prayer. Fr Lourdel, superior of the White Fathers, also tried to intercede with the Kabaka, but to no avail: a few days later the Anglicans received the news that their bishop and all his party had been speared to death. Mwanga then spent several weeks working himself up into an ever greater fury over his majordomo's courageous stand against him. Finally, he ordered Joseph Mukasa executed. The executioners tried to drag their feet, hoping that Mwanga would change his mind, but the Katikiro intervened and sent them a peremptory order to get on with it. The Katikiro was an important and powerful official, and a diehard traditionalist with a profound hatred for the new religious ideas, which he was determined to stamp out. A reprieve did indeed arrive from the Kabaka, but by then it was too late.

Urgent requests for baptism

During the afternoon and evening several groups of pages went to the Catholic mission, saying they expected to be killed too, and asking to be baptised straightaway. The White Fathers agreed, and a number of baptisms were conferred that day and early the following morning. Among those baptised then were Lwanga (given the name Charles), Ssebuggwawo (Denis) and the royal gunsmith Kisule (Matthew). Contrary to their expectations, the situation then seemed to calm down. However three of the younger and prettier pages - Muggaga and Gyavira, and Kizito - found themselves living a constant nightmare trying to avoid the Kabaka's advances. Little Kizito kept begging to be baptised, for fear he wouldn't survive much longer. He began staging sit-ins at the mission, on one occasion spending the whole night there, saying he wouldn't leave until the date was fixed for his baptism. Another time Fr Lourdel picked him up and pushed him out through a window, but in early May 1886, he gave in and promised that Kizito could be baptised in a month's time.

On 25th May the Kabaka arrived home earlier than expected from an unsuccessful hunting trip, in a foul mood, and wanted to know where his pages were. Someone mentioned having seen sixteen-year-old Denis Ssebuggwawo on the road, together with a younger boy named Mwafu, and this triggered a fearful outburst of rage. Mwafu, the Katikiro's son, was very good-looking, and he'd never objected to the Kabaka's sexual attentions, so was a firm favourite. Mwanga suspected the pair were heading for Matthew Kisule's home, which had become a safe space near the court for all the Christian converts, both Catholic and Anglican. Mwanga knew he couldn't touch Kisule, whose skills were essential and irreplaceable, but he wasn't happy about his pages going to Kisule's house, and he certainly did not want Mwafu to become a Christian. The two boys soon came running in, and Mwanga demanded to know what they'd been doing, whereupon Mwafu replied that Ssebuggwawo had been teaching him religion. Mwanga went berserk. He seized a spear and beat Ssebuggwawo with it until it broke, then called for the executioners to take him out and kill him.

Night of fear

The rest of the Catholic pages spent the night together, praying. Charles Lwanga baptised Muggaga, Gyavira and Kizito, and another lad named Mbaga Tuzinde. One of the older pages currently under instruction, Kiriwawanvu, could not be baptised because he wasn't with the others; he'd been put in prison a little while before, at the Kabaka's orders, for losing his temper and hitting Gyavira. Lwanga reassured the terrified Kizito, saying, "When the decisive moment comes, I will take your hand like this. If we have to die for Jesus, we will die together, hand in hand."

Early next morning, around 6am, Mwanga called his chiefs together and began haranguing them. They were all terrified into agreeing that the pages should be put to death and replaced with others - though most of them secretly resolved to do whatever they could to rescue the ones who were related to them. Mwanga then summoned all his pages to his private courtyard. As they arrived and prostrated themselves before him, he sat taunting them and complaining that they were disobedient servants. Then he ordered all those who were Christians to go and stand over by the fence. Lwanga stood up: "You, Sire, are always telling us that we must do our duty, and you know that we have never shirked it despite the threats of our enemies. Today then, once again, we take up the position you command." Taking Kizito by the hand, he walked over to the fence. A number of others joined them there. The Kabaka screamed, "I am going to burn you all!" The Christian pages were all roped together and led outside, ready to be taken to Namugongo.

Executions

The Katikiro was rubbing his hands with glee at how the situation was developing, but he was not satisfied: he insisted that the older Christian leaders also be dealt with - especially the bandmaster-general. The Kabaka greatly valued Andrew Kaggwa's drumming expertise, but was induced to order that officers be sent to Kigowa to arrest Kaggwa and take him to the Katikiro's compound. After a brief interrogation, the Katikiro handed him over to the executioners, saying, "Be quick about it, and bring me his arm to show that you have done your work. I will not touch food until I have seen it." Kaggwa, his face shining, urged the executioners to go ahead, pointing that they would otherwise be in trouble with the Katikiro. So they took him a little way into the bush and made him lie down, and while he lay praying they cut off his arm at the shoulder, then cut off his head and chopped his body into pieces.

Kiriwawanvu was brought out from prison to join the other Christian pages. He knew nothing of what had happened until the executioners told him they were all under sentence of death, and that this also applied to him. "I am grateful to the Kabaka for condemning me thus," he declared. I am anxious to die for my religion." "Well done, my friend!" cried Gyavira, welcoming him rapturously. "Thank you for praying for me," said Kiriwawanvu. "No longer shall we quarrel about our little affairs, but fight together for God." As evening fell they were all marched off. As was customary, some of them were killed at intervals along the route. The sight of dismembered victims of the Kabaka's vengeance was seen as a salutary means of keeping the population properly cowed.

Next day a royal messenger arrived to take Kalemba to the Katikiro. "What has induced a man of your standing to adopt the white man's religion?" asked the Katikiro. "And at your age too?" "I follow that religion because I wish to." replied Kalemba. "You have sent away all your wives, I am told," sneered the Katikiro. "So you cook your own food, I suppose?" Kalemba remained perfectly calm. "Is it because I am thin, or because of my religion that I have been brought before you?" The Katikiro flew into a rage. "So you are the people who are content to marry only one woman? And you are trying to persuade other people to agree to this monstrosity!" Then he turned to the executioners and said, "Cut off his hands and feet, tear strips of flesh from his back and roast them before his eyes; let God deliver him!" Still Kalemba refused to be frightened: "Indeed, God will deliver me, but you will not see how he does it. He will take my soul and leave you my body." The executioners carried out the Katikiro's orders with great brutality. Then they carefully bound up Kalemba's wounds and left him to die a slow and lingering death alone in the bush. It took three days, and during that time nobody dared go near him, for fear of sharing his fate.

Martyrdom

On arrival at Namugongo, the Christian pages were kept imprisoned in huts, while a huge pyre was prepared. On 3rd June they were led out to die. There were about thirty altogether: thirteen Catholics, at least nine Anglicans, and some non-Christians who'd been condemned to death for other reasons. To the amazement of the executioners, instead of wailing and lamenting their fate like other victims, the Christians all seemed very cheerful, as if they were going for a marvellous treat. Each young man was wrapped in reed matting and placed on the pyre, which was then set alight. They continued praying softly until they died.

Altogether about a hundred Christians are believed to

have been killed in the persecution in Buganda between late 1885 and early 1887, though only a minority of the names were recorded. Within a year Mwanga's behaviour had become so extreme that the Catholics, the Protestants and the Muslims formed an alliance to depose him. But they then began fighting among themselves, setting off a chain of events which ended with the imposition of British rule in the 1890s. Twenty-two young men officially recognised as Catholic martyrs were canonised by Pope Paul VI in 1964.

O Jesus, our Lord and Redeemer, through your passion and death, we adore and thank you.

Holy Mary, Mother and Queen of Martyrs, obtain for us sanctification through our sufferings.

St Joseph Mukasa Balikuddembe, first martyr of Uganda, obtain for us a spirit of truth and justice

St Charles Lwanga, guide and protector of young people, obtain for us a firm and zealous faith

St Matthias Kalemba, imitator of Christ meek and humble, obtain for us a Christian gentleness

St Denis Ssebuggwawo, generous friend, obtain for us the courage to share our faith with others

St Andrew Kaggwa, catechist and teacher, obtain for us a love of the teachings of Christ

St Kizito, child resplendent in purity and Christian joy, obtain for us the gift of joy in our Lord

St Gyavira, shining example of how to forgive and forget injuries, obtain for us the grace to forgive

St Mukasa Kiriwawanvu, baptised in your own blood, obtain for us perseverance unto death

St Pontian Ngondwe, pray for us

St Athanasius Bazzekuketta, pray for us

St Gonzaga Gonza, pray for us

St Noah Mwaggali, pray for us

St Luke Banabakintu, pray for us

St James Buzabaliwawo, pray for us

St Ambrose Kibuka, pray for us

St Anatolius Kiriggwajjo, pray for us

St Achilles Kiwanuka, pray for us

St Mbaga Tuzinde, pray for us

St Mugagga, pray for us

St Adolphus Mukasa Ludigo, pray for us

St Bruno Serunkuma, pray for us

St John Muzeyi, pray for us

Holy Martyrs, firm in your fidelity, help us to be always faithful to the true Church of Christ.

Let us pray

O Lord Jesus Christ, who wonderfully strengthened the Holy Martyrs of Uganda, and gave them to us as examples of faith and fortitude, chastity and charity, grant, we beseech you, that by their intercession the same virtues may increase in us, and that we may deserve to become propagators of the true faith. Who lives and reigns world without end. Amen.

Blessed Victoria Rasoamanarivo

Blessed Victoria Rasoamanarivo

King Radama I, ruler of Imerina in the central highlands of Madagascar, signed a treaty with Great Britain in 1817 promising to abolish the slave trade. In return he gained the money and munitions he needed to bring under his rule virtually the whole of the island, one of the world's largest. He happily encouraged British Protestant missionaries to come to Imerina and start schools for the children, and on the face of it seemed very open to modern ideas. Contemporary western observers, who had a habit of glamourising strong rulers, appeared oblivious to the ruthlessness with which he pursued his wars, or the fact that his subjects were obliged to serve him for nothing, whether as military conscripts or in forced labour projects. The nobility also served without pay, but in government positions which provided plenty of opportunity to squeeze everyone else for personal profit.

Radama I's successor, Queen Ranavalona, expelled the missionaries and persecuted their converts - though the persecutions were intermittent, and the Malagasy Christians continued to worship in secret. There was no question of rejecting everything foreign. Jean Laborde, a Frenchman who was shipwrecked off the coast, received a warm welcome at the royal court. The son of a blacksmith with a wide range of practical skills, he helped the government develop some simple industries, including state factories for firearms production. No wages had to be paid, because the factories were staffed with forced labour.

French Catholic missionaries worked meanwhile with Malagasy people living on other islands, including small ones off the coast of Madagascar where Queen Ranavalona's writ did not run: they thereby acquired a good knowledge of the language and culture. In 1855 another French entrepreneur, Joseph-François Lambert, arrived at Anantanarivo, the Imerina capital. There his good offices secured entrée to the royal court for three associates, all of whom were actually Jesuits in disguise. Their stay was necessarily brief, but they established friendly relations with the heir apparent. This young prince also signed a charter granting Lambert the right to develop all the forests, minerals and unoccupied land in Madagascar in return for a ten per cent royalty to the government, and sent a letter to Napoleon III requesting a French protectorate. From his viewpoint this made perfectly good sense. As queen, his mother was regarded with deep reverence by the whole population, but politically she was a mere figurehead: all the real power lay with an oligarchy of high-ranking officials and army officers. An alliance with France, even on unfavourable terms, might enable the monarchy to outflank the oligarchy.

The return of the Jesuits

In 1861 the old queen died. The Jesuits, who were eagerly awaiting the news, returned immediately. They received a warm welcome from the former prince, who was now King Radama II, and practical assistance from Laborde. Everyone could see which way the wind was blowing, and when two Sisters of St Joseph of Cluny arrived to start a school, the very highest families brought their daughters to be enrolled. Soon the Sisters were running one class for well-born girls and another for slaves. When one of the priests fell ill the prime minister's fourteen-year-old niece, Rasoamanarivo, volunteered to take over the teaching of catechism to the slaves.

Radama II only reigned for a couple of years before the oligarchy staged a coup, deposed and murdered him, and replaced him with his wife who became Queen Rasoherina. However this led to no immediate changes in religious policy. When the first baptism of Catholic converts took place on 1st November 1863, almost all the candidates were young girls who were pupils at the Sisters' school. Each one was given a saint's name, and Rasoamanarivo became Victoire (Victoria). She was an extraordinarily well-connected young lady. The prime minister, Rainilaiarivony, was her maternal uncle, and he'd quite quickly married the queen, thereby making himself also prince consort. Her paternal uncle Rainimaharavo (who was her legal guardian, since her father had died) was secretary of state, and her mother was a lady-in-waiting.

Marriage

Elite Malagasy families were always complicatedly intermarried, and at sixteen she married her cousin, Rainilaiarivony's eldest son, Radriaka. It was an arranged marriage and Radriaka wasn't a Christian, but Rasoamanarivo insisted they have a Catholic ceremony as well as a traditional wedding. After her marriage she continued to attend the Sisters' school. The Lasallian Brothers arrived in 1866 and opened a boys' school, and once again the pupils included sons of officials, though not of the highest rank. Among the first to enrol was a lad named Firinga. The name actually meant "dustbin": this was in accordance with a custom, common in many cultures, of giving children pejorative names as a way of warding off ill fortune.

The Malagasy government repudiated Lambert's charter, but was obliged to pay France 1,200,000 francs as compensation. This created ill-feeling against the French and, because Catholicism was seen as a French religion, also against Catholicism. The prime minister's family began veering towards Protestantism, and transferring their children to Protestant schools. Rasoamanarivo was dragged to her new school by force, but once there she just sat and cried. She formed an alliance with one of the house slaves, a woman named Rosalie who was a firm Catholic though still a catechumen, and went with her morning and evening to the church to pray the rosary. After three days the teacher had had enough and refused to keep her in the Protestant school, so she was allowed to return to the Sisters.

Queen Ranavalona II, who ascended the throne in 1868, refused to allow any traditional religious ceremonies at her coronation. Shortly afterwards she and Rainilaiarivony, who'd promptly married her and so was still prince consort as well as prime minister, announced their decision to be baptised. The queen made a bonfire of the royal *sampy* (sacred cult objects), and declared Christianity the state religion. Everyone was supposed to be free to follow whatever religion they preferred, but "the Queen's religion", which was a Congregationalist-style Protestantism, enjoyed the greatest social cachet, and Catholics complained of experiencing considerable pressure to accept it.

The Queen's Religion

Radriaka, quoting the words of St Paul about the husband being the head of the wife, told Rasoamanarivo it was her duty to join "the Queen's religion" as he'd done. She ignored him. Radriaka was at heart thoroughly irreligious, a heavy drinker and a womaniser. When he came home sober she'd sit him down and wash his feet - a task ordinarily assigned to a slave - and she never complained or nagged him, though she'd talk seriously to him about what he was doing to himself. It occasionally happened that he went to the extreme of bringing one of his mistresses home, but that was rare: more often he was carried home dead drunk, in which case Rasoamanarivo would look after him and put him to bed. Both the queen and the prime minister found Radriaka's behaviour so shocking that they advised Roasoamanarivo to divorce him, but she replied: "The teaching of the Gospel is clear. 'What God has united, man must not divide'". An added sadness was that she was unable to have children.

Rather than letting her difficult marriage situation poison her life, Rasoamanarivo found plenty of other things to do, and she always seemed happy and cheerful. She used to get up every morning at 3am and spend some time praying, kneeling at a *prie dieu* in front of the large altar by her bed. She then set off for the big Church of the Immaculate Conception, which opened at 4am, escorted by a single slave holding a lantern. The slave said a quick prayer and then went home, returning to fetch her at 8am. Rasoamanarivo remained in the church for all the morning Masses, in between which she prayed quietly by the Lady Altar. Once the day was properly started she went off to attend to her various practical and social duties as mistress of an important man's household, and at the palace. She also found time to visit the poor and sick, distribute alms to beggars, prisoners and lepers, and interview supplicants in desperate need of someone to intervene for them with the authorities - for example, families whose sole breadwinner had been drafted into the army. At 3pm she returned to the church for two hours' adoration before the Blessed Sacrament, and at 6pm she assembled her house slaves for evening prayers and recitation of the Rosary. She herself often continued praying alone in her room later in the evening, especially the night before First Fridays when the slaves who slept in the room adjoining sometimes heard her still praying as late as midnight. Wherever she went, she kept her rosary with her, and prayed it at any opportunity.

Growth of Christianity

Like all her family she had considerable personal wealth, and owned hundreds of slaves. Freeing them was not really an option: slaves were chary of emancipation, because they were often better off as they were than as free peasants liable to forced labour for the state. So she ensured they were all properly looked after, the children sent to school, and any who fell ill provided with medical care. Her house slaves were devoted to her, and she could rely on them to run her household with a minimum of supervision. The slaves who worked her fields were not expected to supply her with rice for free, and if she needed them to do any extra work she paid them a fair wage. She followed a simple and frugal lifestyle, eating the same meals as her slaves, and drinking only water. It had become fashionable at court to wear western clothes, and those who could afford it built up expensive wardrobes, but Rasoamanarivo preferred to stick to traditional clothing.

The Protestant churches acquired hundreds of thousands of adherents, and most upper-class Christians chose to be Protestant. But Catholic numbers also grew steadily, and a few Malagasy girls applied to join the Sisters of St Joseph. In 1876 Firinga applied to become a Lasallian Brother, and a year later he was clothed in the habit, becoming Brother Raphael Rafiringa. (The "Ra" particle is an honorific.) The churches provided Madagascar with an education system by running basic primary schools on the Lancasterian plan, whereby older children were deployed as monitors to teach the younger ones: even the relatively small Catholic community deployed over 500 teachers. Attendance at schools run directly by the teaching religious, which offered a higher standard of education, was a privilege which could only be extended to limited numbers, and their former pupils were the elite of the Catholic community. About forty of the better educated young men were invited to form a Catholic Union, while the Sisters enrolled Rasoamanarivo and their other old girls as Children of Mary. By the early 1880s there were 80,000 Malagasy Catholics, though very few were of high rank, and a great many were slaves. Besides the Immaculate Conception, a whole network of smaller churches, chapels and Mass centres had been established.

A guardian angel to the Catholics

On Laborde's death his extensive property in Madagascar, instead of going to his heirs, was confiscated in the queen's name. This injustice to a French national infuriated his home government, and in May 1883 the French navy seized the port of Mahajanga, on the north-west coast. Immediately all the French missionaries were ordered to leave the country. When Rasoamanarivo went to say goodbye to her parish priest, he told her she must be a guardian angel to the Catholics while the missionaries were gone. She promised to do her best. The Lasallian superior gave similar instructions to Brother Raphael.

Three days later it was Sunday. The Catholics wanted to go to their churches, even if the Blessed Sacrament had been removed and there could be no Mass, but they found the doors shut and guards posted outside, with registers to write down the names of anyone who asked to go in. Rasoamanarivo sized up the situation outside the Church of the Immaculate Conception. If this was a case of some official exceeding his instructions, it could and should be challenged. But first she went quickly to the palace to confirm the order did not come from the top. She then walked calmly up to the door and declared: "You can put me to death, but you have no right to shut the church." Taken aback, the guards opened the doors, Rasoamanarivo went in and everyone else followed.

Shortly afterwards Brother Raphael arrived, dressed in his religious habit, and led his schoolchildren in. A planning meeting was held in the church to decide what to do next. Rasoamanarivo advised that they organise a programme of religious devotions and catechetical talks, starting with the churches in Anantanarivo and then going out to the countryside. Finally Brother Raphael was called on to lead the congregation in prayer. A further meeting was held in the afternoon, at which the Catholic Union elected Brother Raphael to be their president.

In June the French occupied the port of Toamasina on the east coast. In July Queen Ranavalona II died; her successor took the name Ranavalona III, and in her turn married Rainilaiarivony. In anticipation of a full-scale French invasion, an order was issued for all fit men to do military training, so Brother Raphael obediently began drilling his pupils, and provided a well-trained guard of honour for the queen at her coronation. From September onwards, Catholic Union members were allocated to each of the mission districts round the capital to lead Sunday services. Rasoamanarivo's support and advice remained essential because of her social standing, the respect in which she was held in the Catholic community, and her quiet common sense. She often attended the Catholic Union's weekly planning meetings, and stood ready to help in a crisis. Brother Raphael, while continuing to run the boys' school, recruited and trained additional catechists, and organised retreats for the six Malagasy Sisters, none of whom was as yet professed. In the event there was no invasion and not much serious fighting, and when in 1886 the dispute with France was settled and the missionaries returned, they found the Catholic Church of Madagascar in better condition than before.

Bereavement and Death

On the night of 9th March 1888, news came to Rasoamanarivo that Radriaka had had a serious accident. He'd fallen from a nearby house, almost certainly while on one of his philandering expeditions, and broken several ribs. At once she summoned porters and went to fetch him, arranged for the best possible medical care, and nursed him personally over the next four days, but it was clear he could not recover. Her deepest concern was for her husband's salvation. They'd been married for twenty-five years, and all that time she'd been praying for him, and her prayers at last bore fruit: he asked to become a Catholic. She sent for the priest, but he couldn't come in time, so she baptised him herself. A few minutes later he died.

Rasoamanarivo wore mourning for her husband for the rest of her life. She died on 21st August 1894, after a four-day illness. During the last hour she clung to her crucifix and rosary, asking those around her to pray for her, and as she died she lifted up the rosary and called, "Mother, Mother, Mother!"

Brother Raphael's trial

Madagascar had tried to play France and Britain off against each other, but without lasting success: the two powers reached an agreement that, in return for allowing Britain a free hand in Zanzibar, France could have Madagascar. Accordingly Madagascar became a French colony in 1896, and the monarchy was abolished. The Malagasy had no choice but to adapt to the new situation. Brother Raphael began running French language classes for young people, and a course in Malagasy culture for people coming in from France. He started a magazine to educate outsiders about Malagasy culture and traditions.

During the First World War Brother Raphael's well-known patriotism got him into trouble with the French authorities: they suspected him of being involved with a Malagasy nationalist plot to take advantage of the global conflict to stage a coup and declare independence. He was arrested on Christmas Eve 1915 and thrown into a filthy underground cell, and the interrogations began shortly after midnight on Christmas morning. But when the case came to trial, it became clear there was no evidence against him: the judge actually apologised and ordered his immediate release. The following day Brother Raphael went to the Bishop and asked if he could let him have a new rosary: the one he'd had with him in prison was completely worn out. Though happy to be free, his two months' prison experience had shattered his health, so the Lasallian Brothers retired him. He died on 19th May 1919, aged sixty-three.

Victoria Rasoamanarivo was beatified in 1989, and Brother Raphael in 2009.

Blessed Victoria Rasoamanarivo, through God's grace your spiritual motherhood was fruitful beyond all measure. Help us by, your example and intercession, to be faithful to our baptismal calling, and to carry out the special mission God has planned for each one of us. Through Christ our Lord. Amen.

Blessed Raphael Rafiringa, through your docility to the Holy Spirit, you were able to guide others along the path of faith and love. Obtain for us the grace to be illuminated with the truth, and ready for service of our brothers. Through Christ our Lord. Amen.

Blessed Isidore Bakanja

Blessed Isidore Bakanja

The most extraordinary of all the outcomes of the 1884-85 Berlin Congress, at which the European powers agreed ground rules for sharing out Africa among themselves, was that Leopold II, King of the Belgians, was awarded the whole of the Congo Basin to be his personal possession. He undertook to eradicate the slave trade throughout the region, and promote the economic development of what he called the "Congo Free State", under free market conditions, for the benefit of European entrepreneurs of all nations, and equally for the benefit of the people who lived there. At the time, it sounded plausible. It was well known that Leopold had been busy sponsoring exploration of the Congo, and he'd also encouraged missionaries, both Protestant and Catholic, to establish themselves there, and help sway public opinion in their home countries in his favour.

What Leopold actually did was to allocate vast expanses of African land as "concessions" to specially created companies, while reserving equally vast areas for himself as "Crown Domain." Both the company agents, and Leopold's administrators, exercised monopoly rights in exploiting their land grants, and relied heavily on forced labour, enforcing discipline with vicious rawhide whips. Initially the companies were planning to hunt elephants for ivory, but they quickly switched to rubber. Demand for rubber in industrialised countries was soaring, and the cultivation of rubber trees on large plantations was only just beginning: it would take time for the young trees to reach maturity, and meanwhile the only source was from the rubber trees which still grew wild in some parts of the world - central Africa being one. The companies in the Congo drove local people into the jungle to search for rubber vines and harvest the raw rubber for export to Europe. Huge quotas were set, and failure to fulfil the quotas was punished by terror tactics: villages and food crops were destroyed, and men, women and children killed or mutilated. By the turn of the century fat profits were flowing to Leopold and the shareholders of the various companies, among the most successful of which was the Société Anonyme Belge (SAB).

Campaign for reform

It might be surprising to learn that large numbers of Africans freely volunteered to work for the Europeans, but they did. Even with advanced weaponry, there was no way a very small number of European personnel could have subjugated an estimated thirty million Africans without indigenous allies. The various ethnic groups and local communities inhabiting the Congo rarely had qualms about fighting each other, so men readily enlisted as soldiers or security guards. But there were also plenty of peaceful and constructive jobs available that paid reasonable wages. Moreover many Congolese had positive experiences with the missionaries. Although the missionaries were chary of speaking out about what was going on, they did try to protect the Africans against the companies, and for this reason many of the company personnel became bitterly anti-Christian in their attitude.

The atrocities in the Congo began at last to be exposed by a Liverpool-based human rights campaigner, Edmund Morel. Roger Casement was then sent on a fact-finding mission by the British government to establish whether Morel's allegations were true, and his report, published in 1904, confirmed that they were. Europe was rocked by the scandal.

Bakanja's conversion

It was around 1904 that a young lad named Bakanja decided to leave his home village of Bokendela, on the banks of the River Botato, and travel in a trading canoe downriver to the colonial settlement of Coquilhatville (Mbandaka) to look for work. He was then about sixteen. Coquilhatville was expanding rapidly, with buildings going up everywhere, and Bakanja was quickly taken on as an assistant stonemason. He was intrigued to discover that a number of his workmates were Christians. Every Sunday

they all set off for Mass at Boloko Wa Nsimba, and he
asked if he could go too. The Belgian Trappists and team
of African catechists who staffed the chapel had thousands
of catechumens under instruction, and on average there
were thirty baptisms each Sunday. It was an hour's walk
there and back, but Bakanja decided it was well worth the
effort, and quite soon he asked to become a Christian too.
He was baptised in May 1906, and his catechist, Boniface
Bankutu, chose Isidore as his baptismal name. The priest
presented him with a scapular, and told him it was very
important always to wear it: that way, everyone would
know he was a Christian.

When Bakanja's contract ended he returned to his village,
but quite soon set out again for more work experience.
This time he travelled upriver to the town of Busira,
which was the main SAB station, and found employment
as houseboy to an SAB agent named Reynders. He
enjoyed his new job, and Reynders seemed reasonable and
pleasant. So when - towards the end of 1908 - Reynders
was appointed assistant manager to the Ikili rubber estate,
Bakanja ignored the warning of a fellow-houseboy and
accompanied him to Ikili. Meanwhile Leopold had been
induced to transfer control of the Congo to Belgium, but
nothing much changed in the short term - especially within
the company concessions, where the company agents were
a law unto themselves.

A martyr for the scapular

At Ikili, Reynders was second-in-command to the manager André Van Cauter, a sadistic character who strutted round the estate brandishing an elephant-hide whip studded with nails, though he'd not so far actually used it on anyone. Bakanja soon discovered that none of the other estate employees was a Christian. Some of them asked him questions about his faith, but this sent Van Cauter into a rage. The sight of Bakanja's scapular infuriated him even further, and he ordered the boy to take it off. Van Cauter had a visceral hatred of Christianity, and believed that allowing Africans to practise Christianity would only encourage them to get above themselves. He forbade Bakanja to pray anywhere on the plantation, even in his own time, so Bakanja used to go along the path to the neighbouring village to say the rosary. He asked to be allowed to give up his job and return to his village, but for that he needed a pass letter from Van Cauter, and the manager wouldn't give him one. He'd pushed his scapular well down under his shirt, but he wouldn't take it off - not even when Van Cauter, spotting the string sticking out, had him whipped for not obeying his order.

A few days later, on 2nd February 1909, the houseboys served lunch to the two Ikili managers and another who was visiting. Afterwards they cleared up, and left the managers sitting round the table. Suddenly Van Cauter began calling for Bakanja, and sent someone to fetch him. Accusing him of going off to pray, the Belgian tore the scapular off the boy's neck, threw him on the ground and ordered one of the headmen to flog him with the elephant-hide whip. He himself kept screaming at him, kicking him on the head and hitting him with an axe handle, and yelling at the horrified headman to continue the flogging. After 200-250 blows Bakanja's entire back was laid open, raw and bleeding. He was then dragged off to a shed, chained up and left there. Three days later Van Cauter recalled that an inspection was imminent, so he'd need to get Bakanja out of sight. He ordered Reynders off to another part of the plantation, and told the houseboy to go with him. Bakanja was still unable to walk, but Van Cauter threatened to have him whipped again, so he dragged himself away as best he could. But instead of following Reyners, he hid on the edge of the estate, and stayed there until the morning of 7th February, when Inspector Dörpinghaus arrived and found him. Inspectors in the Congo were all too often only interested in a quiet life, but Dörpinghaus was a man of integrity. He took Bakanja away to safety and arranged for him to be cared for, and had Van Cauter dismissed.

For the next six months Bakanja lay helpless, and by July his wounds were badly infected, and giving him severe pain. Just then two Trappist missionaries arrived in Busira, and were taken to see him. They gave him the Last Rites, and he told them what had happened, but added

"I'm not angry with the white man. If he beat me that's his problem, not mine. If I die, I'll pray for him in heaven."

Isidore Bakanja died on 15th August 1909. He was beatified in 1994, and is considered a martyr of the scapular.

Blessed Isidore Bakanja, despite mockery and persecution you persevered to the shedding of blood, forgave your enemies, and went to heaven on the Feast of the Assumption of Our Lady, whose scapular you faithfully wore. Help us, by your example and intercession, to forgive those who have injured us, to pray for our enemies and love those who hurt us. Through Christ our Lord. Amen.

Blessed Daudi Okelo and Blessed Jildo Irwa

Blessed Daudi Okelo and Blessed Jildo Irwa

The Acholi people of northern Uganda were divided into clans, each under its own chief, and had no centralised government. The system worked well enough until the mid-nineteenth century, when outsiders began coming into their area. The first to arrive were slavers from Egyptian-occupied Sudan, and they were followed by Ethiopian elephant hunters. Both groups enlisted Acholi to help them in their raids, and gave them guns. But as more and more locals acquired guns, wars began breaking out between neighbouring chiefs. Most of the outsiders the Acholi were initially in contact with were Muslims, so a few of them converted to Islam. From 1903, when the first Protestant missionaries arrived, a few others adopted Christianity, but on the whole the Acholi stuck to their traditional beliefs and showed little interest in other religions. Northern Uganda was seen as having very little economic potential, and the British colonial officials, who were busy consolidating their control over the prosperous south, were inclined to leave the north largely to its own devices. However the growing violence in Acholi, which threatened to have a destabilising impact on surrounding areas, caused them to think again.

Meanwhile the Comboni Fathers, who already had considerable experience of working with Acholi people in South Sudan, decided to expand their operations across the border into northern Uganda to work with the Acholi there. On 30th December 1909 the missionaries assigned for the task set off from Khartoum, travelling in a steamboat as far as it could go up the Nile, then continuing their journey on foot. The year they arrived, 1910, was the same year the British established a station at Gulu, and began considering how to bring the region under firmer control. Two years later they founded a second station at Kitgum, in eastern Acholi.

Catechesis

To help them get started the Comboni Fathers borrowed African catechists from southern Uganda, where the Catholic communities were already well established, but as soon as possible they began training local Acholi catechists. By the time a branch mission was started at Kitgum, in February 1915, most of the people living around the new base had at least heard of the "people from Khartoum." Four experienced catechists had arrived well in advance of the white missionaries, among them Bonifacio Okot who was to be the chief catechist based in Kitgum. One of the others, named Antonio, was posted to Paimol, a chiefdom fifty miles away.

Fr Cesare Gambaretto began travelling around the villages near Kitgum. The Acholi were surprised that a white man wanted to join them as they sat round the fire in the evening, after the day's work, telling stories, but they welcomed him politely. He would sit there praying the Rosary, and using the Mysteries to talk about the life of Jesus. The children loved listening to him, and he invited them to start coming together for regular meetings in their villages for what were known as "morning lessons." Youngsters who completed the morning lessons were given holy medals to wear, and invited to begin their catechumenate.

Conversions

Among the first to reach the catechumenate stage were two young lads named Okelo and Irwa. Okelo was born in 1900 to a couple named Lode and Amona, in the village of Ogom-Payira which stood on a well-used caravan route. He was a cousin of the catechist Antonio. Irwa, whose name means "ours", was born two years later in Bar-Kitoba. His mother Ato died when he was very young, and his father Tongfur married again, but Irwa's stepmother Akelo thought the world of him. As Irwa grew older he acquired four little half-sisters, but he remained the only boy in the family. The catechumenate period was spent at Kitgum: the boys all slept in huts near the mission, and were given jobs to do: Irwa worked in the scullery at the Sisters' house. They met together for "evening lessons" and learned by heart the Catechism of St Pius X in an Acholi translation. In June 1916 Okelo and Irwa were baptised by Fr Cesare, and each given a crucifix and a saint's name: Okelo, who was then 16, became Daudi (David), while 14-year-old Irwa was given the name Ermenegildo, which he used in the shortened form "Jildo". The two were confirmed on 15th October the same year, and began training as catechists.

Teaching the faith

Early in 1917 Antonio died. Daudi and Jildo went to Fr Cesare and asked, "Who will go to Paimol to replace Antonio?" At a catechists' meeting in November they volunteered to go themselves. Fr Cesare warned them it might be dangerous, but Daudi said if they were killed, they'd go to heaven. Jildo said, "Father, do not be afraid, Jesus and Mary are with us." They knelt and recited a Hail Mary, and Fr Cesare gave them his blessing, conducting a short commissioning rite to show that they were sent in the name of the Church. Bonifacio Okot then escorted them to a village in Paimol named Palamuku, where he presented them as the new catechists. The sub-chief, Ogal, arranged for them to live in a hut next to that of his brother Ocok. He also offered to provide free meals, but they said they wanted to work for their keep.

Every morning before sunrise Daudi used to beat the drum to call people to come for morning prayers, and a short period of instruction, before he and Jildo went to the fields to work. Later they assembled the children for a catechism class, and before bedtime they prayed the rosary. The children loved their sessions with Daudi and Jildo, and many of the adults - especially the younger men - were keen to know more. The catechists also visited the elderly and sick, and people who had problems started coming to them to talk things over and seek advice. But some of the villagers grew uneasy, seeing these new ideas as a challenge to their traditional way of life.

Drought and disease

Times were hard in Acholi due a drought which had set in a year or so previously, and was already leading to serious food shortages. A particularly vicious strain of venereal disease had become prevalent in the region, and then came outbreaks of smallpox and Spanish flu. Meanwhile British rule was bringing additional burdens, without any corresponding benefits that anyone could see: everyone was obliged to pay a poll tax, supposedly in money, but because most of the local people weren't part of the money economy they were liable to be drafted for forced labour in lieu of payment. Before, some people had acquired wealth through working for the slave traders, but the British had prohibited the slave trade. The Acholi also resented having to register their firearms, and being pushed around by flunkeys brought in from southern Uganda, who looked down on the northerners as savages. To "pacify" the region, the British then began deposing the traditional village chiefs and putting in their own nominees, not realising that this only fuelled the unrest. Chief Lakidi of Paimol was arrested and sent to prison, and a man named Amet appointed in his stead. Lakidi's sentence, which he served at Kitgum, was quite short, and while in prison he behaved compliantly to conciliate the authorities. He returned to Paimol expecting to take up the reins again, only for Amet to raise fresh accusations against him. That was the last straw: he fled to the bush to join up with other Acholi who were organising an armed uprising.

Rumours had been spreading for some time that it must be the new religion, Christianity, that was bringing misfortune upon Paimol. These rumours were fostered by those who had particular reasons for seeing the catechists as a threat to their own agendas: specialist practitioners in the traditional religion, who feared a loss of custom, and also some of the local Muslims. So it wasn't difficult to persuade the insurgents to include Daudi in their hit list. Ogal, who was seething because he'd also been demoted and replaced, agreed that the catechist should be killed.

Martyrdom

On the evening of Saturday 19th October 1918 Daudi and Jildo prayed the Rosary with their catechumens and then went to bed. But in the early hours of Sunday morning, long before dawn, a band of armed men approached and split into three groups. One headed for Amet's house, planning to assassinate him, and another headed for the home of the newly-appointed sub-chief who'd replaced Ogal. The third group, a handpicked contingent of men from Palamuku who knew the catechists, crept towards their hut. Ocok spotted them and guessed why they'd come. He argued with them that it was bad luck to kill someone in a house where they'd been welcomed and had eaten food. Daudi, who'd been woken by the voices, came out to see what was going on, and Ocok gestured to him to run, but he wouldn't. One of the attackers, Okiki Ibrahim, then grabbed him and took him outside the village fence. He commanded him to give up his Christian faith, but Daudi refused, and Okiki speared him. The attackers had assumed it wouldn't be necessary to kill the younger catechist as well, but Jildo came out of the hut and shouted to them, "If you killed Daudi because he taught the new religion, kill me too." Another attacker, Opio, ran him through with a spear and finished him off with a knife.

The killers warned the villagers not to bury the bodies, or they'd be killed too, and to have nothing more to do with Christianity. A few days later some of them went and tied ropes round the boys' necks, and dragged them further away from the village, leaving them next to an abandoned termite hill. Thanks to this natural marker, it was possible in 1926 to identify and recover their remains, which were taken to Kitgum to be buried at the foot of the Sacred Heart altar in the church. They were beatified in 2002.

Blessed Daudi and Jildo, in your hearts burned an ardent desire to proclaim the Gospel, and through your martyrdom you strengthened the early growth of the Church in your homeland. Help us to become strong in our faith, and to share it with our brothers and sisters. Through Christ our Lord. Amen.

Blessed Michael Cyprian Iwene Tansi

Iwene Tansi was born in 1903 in Aguleri, by the River Anambra, not far above where it flows into the Niger: the name Iwene (meaning "let malice not kill") may be a reference to his father's having been unjustly imprisoned a few years previously by the British colonial authorities. His family lived according to the traditional beliefs and customs of the Igbo people, the majority ethnic group in eastern Nigeria. He had two half-brothers, two full brothers, and a sister, none of whom ever went to school. But when Iwene was eight years old Robert Orekyie, a relative on his mother's side who was headmaster of the Catholic school in Aguleri, agreed to sponsor his education.

Iwene went to stay in Orekyie's house. Like all African children he was expected to work for his keep: he did the housework, and in return Orekyie fed, clothed and boarded him. On 7th January 1912 he was baptised, taking the name Michael, and at sixteen he became a pupil teacher. The pupil teacher system, whereby would-be teachers helped out in schools and learned on the job, offered a way for a boy from a poor family to gain higher education and become a fully-fledged white-collar professional. Michael's next teaching post was in the town of Onitsha, and in due course

Blessed Michael Cyprian Iwene Tansi

he passed all his examinations. When he was twenty-one he returned as headmaster of Aguleri school.

Training for the priesthood

Michael's family were very proud of their headmaster son, and they were up in arms when, after less than a year, he announced that he was giving it all up: he was going to Onitsha to train for the priesthood. His widowed mother, Ejikwevi, went to the mission and stormed and raged, demanding her son back. Even Orekyie was annoyed: as the educated one, Michael was supposed to concentrate on his career, earning promotion and higher pay so he could help the rest of the family. He was also supposed to marry and have lots of children. But Michael would not be dissuaded.

He was to spend the next twelve years as a seminarian. The reason it took so long was partly because the missionaries were still in two minds about whether forming African clergy was a good idea, and partly because the mission was so short-staffed. Not until December 1930 was John Cross Anyogu ordained as the very first Nigerian priest. Michael, while pursuing his seminary studies, also taught a mathematics class in the teacher training college nearby. Meanwhile there'd been a family tragedy, but he only got to hear about it some time later. A smallpox epidemic in Aguleri gave rise to accusations against a number of people - among them Ejikwevi - of causing it by witchcraft, and Ejikwevi was forced to drink poison and died. One of the consequences of their mother's murder was that Michael's brothers and sister turned against traditional practices and became Christians.

Michael Tansi was eventually ordained in December 1937. After a first posting as assistant to Fr Anyogu in Nnewi, he became a parish priest, serving in Dumukofia 1940-45, Akpu 1945-49 and Aguleri 1949-50. He was never universally popular: on one occasion a group of his wealthiest and most important parishioners wrote to the bishop asking for him to be transferred elsewhere, because "he was too much for God's Law and wasn't interested in what they wanted." Nor did Fr Tansi manifest any of the personal qualities that people are usually thinking of when they speak of "charisma". Nevertheless many of his parishioners were convinced he was a living saint, and he inspired numerous vocations to the priesthood; the future Cardinal Francis Arinze, who was baptised by Fr Tansi on his ninth birthday, always said he'd decided to become a priest "to be like him." Though in many respects a very ordinary, unimpressive, matter-of-fact kind of person, Fr Tansi lived his life in a way so totally dedicated to God as to make it quite extraordinary.

Work and prayer

From childhood he'd developed the habit of spending long periods in church praying, but virtually every waking moment that wasn't devoted to prayer found him hard at work. Each of his parishes covered a vast area, with a central mission and a great many outstations, at each of which Mass must be celebrated at least once a month. So just cycling or walking round the parish was hard work and time-consuming, but that didn't worry him, and when people complained about the long walk to Mass, he put them to shame by leaving his bicycle at home and walking there too. He didn't need much time for meals, because he hardly ate anything: nobody could understand how he kept body and soul together on such a meagre diet. The parishes were still in their early stages, and a lot of his effort necessarily went into expanding and maintaining the material infrastructure of churches and chapels, schools, staff housing and all the other ancillary buildings without which nothing else could be achieved. During the Second World War concrete was in short supply, so he used traditional materials: mud and thatch. Everyone happily volunteered to help, because they saw he had no objection to getting his own hands dirty and toiling in the heat of the sun. Whatever needed doing - clearing the bush, fetching water from the river, making mud blocks - he worked alongside the volunteers. When the women came to scrub the floors, he scrubbed with them.

Along with his time and energy, Fr Tansi saw both his own and the parish's money as belonging to God. This applied to how it was spent, and also to how it was raised. All Catholics were liable to pay a lump sum Annual Mission

Contribution, and other fees, which were often a heavy burden for the poorer parishioners. But if Fr Tansi knew someone couldn't afford it, he'd invite them to do some work for the parish in lieu of money, or simply waive the payment. He himself lived very frugally, and all that could be spared of the money that he did raise was distributed to those in need. If his relatives came round asking for money, he refused: if they were really desperate, he offered to pay them a fair wage for a given amount of work.

The vocation of marriage and women's welfare

For himself, Fr Tansi lived his priestly celibacy; for his parishioners, he promoted the vocation of real Christian marriage. If a young man couldn't afford to get married, he'd help him financially. All the young women were encouraged to join the Children of Mary, and every outstation had a branch; every Sunday they walked together to Mass. Both before and after marriage they provided peer support to each other in resisting pressure to engage in pre-marital and extra-marital sexual relations, even in circumstances where such behaviour was sanctioned by custom. They'd intervene in cases of domestic violence, arriving together to rescue the wife and take her to a place of refuge, or else they'd move in with her and remain as a protective presence, eating the husband's yams, until he agreed to treat her better. Fr Tansi used his authority to separate cohabiting couples; he'd take the girl away to follow a residential course in housewifery and Catholic teaching for a period of between two and six months, during which he obliged the man to support her, until Fr Tansi was satisfied the pair were ready to enter into a properly sacramental marriage. This may sound high-handed, but both the men and the women came to accept and value the procedure, because they saw it enabled couples to lay the foundation for a much higher quality of married life.

Fr Tansi was deeply hostile to traditional religious practices, understandably so in view of what had happened to his mother. Among the most colourful were the masquerades, in which Igbo men paraded wearing spirit masks in order to terrify and control women and children. Both boys and girls were led to believe that the masqueraders really were spirits on the move, and whereas the boys when they were old enough were let into the secret, the girls were never supposed to find out. Anyone who dared to touch the masks was supposed to be killed. But Fr Tansi made it clear he wasn't the least afraid of the masquerades: he'd openly confront and challenge them, and had no qualms about identifying the mask-wearers and revealing their secrets. One day in Aguleri a band of Children of Mary confronted a masquerade, and Elizabeth Okwonkwo seized the mask. Furious, the masqueraders began beating her up, but her friends ran to fetch Fr Tansi who came charging down the street on his bicycle and sent them packing. He then encouraged Elizabeth to take them to court, and they were made to pay her compensation. It was a great victory for women's rights!

Life as a monk

Although he made such a good parish priest, Fr Tansi became convinced that his true vocation was to be a contemplative monk. There weren't any monasteries in Africa, so it was arranged for him to go to England. In 1950 he entered the Cistercian Abbey of Mount St Bernard, taking the religious name Cyprian. The idea was for him eventually to return and found a Cistercian Abbey in Nigeria, but things did not work out as planned, and he had to stay in England. The people of Onitsha Diocese did not forget him, and he constantly received letters and visitors from Nigeria in search of advice. Eventually he was selected to go and start a monastery in Cameroon, but before he could leave he was suddenly taken ill. He died in Leicester Royal Infirmary on 20th January 1964.

In 1986 the Bishops of Nigeria brought Fr Tansi's body back to Onitsha to be buried in the cathedral. Pope John Paul II travelled specially to Nigeria in 1998 to perform the beatification ceremony.

Blessed Cyprian Michael Tansi, during your life on earth you showed great faith and love in giving yourself to your people, and in the hidden life of prayer and contemplation. Help us, by your example and intercession, to honour God above all things. Through Christ our Lord. Amen.

Blessed Clementine Alphonsine
Anuarite Nengapeta

Amisi Badjulu and his wife Isude already had three little girls when, on 29th December 1939, a fourth arrived whom they named Nengapeta (meaning "riches deceive"). They lived near Wamba in the north-east of the Belgian Congo. In 1940 the German Army occupied Belgium, but the Congo remained loyal to the Belgian government-in-exile. Amisi was called up to join the Congolese forces fighting on the Allied side in the East African Campaign, and his unit ended up in Palestine, where the life of Jesus Christ came to seem very real to him. So he wrote home to Isude, telling her to go to the Catholic mission and arrange to receive instruction. Isude was duly baptised in 1943, taking the name Julienne. The three younger girls were also baptised, and Nengapeta became Alphonsine.

When Amisi got home he himself began instruction, but he never finished the course because his manager transferred him to another town, and after that he lost interest in Christianity. He was a long-distance lorry driver, and moved around quite a lot. The main family home remained in Wamba, and the children - including two more daughters born after the war - grew up there.

Blessed Clementine Alphonsine Anuarite Nengapeta

Their grandmother Anjelina lived with them. From time to time Julienne and the two eldest girls went and stayed with Amisi for a while, leaving the younger ones with Anjelina; the old woman had become a very committed and devout Catholic, and she was an important influence in Alphonsine's upbringing. Amisi, like all traditional African fathers, wanted a son, but Julienne had only given him six girls, so he took a second wife.

Schooling

There was no school in Wamba until 1948, when the Sisters of the Infant Jesus arrived to start one. Alphonsine was enrolled together with her older sister Leontine Anuarite, but the Sister who registered the girls made a mistake, and registered them both as Anuarite. Alphonsine didn't make a fuss, and soon got used to being called Anuarite (meaning "she scorns war"). She also had to get used to being taught in French, instead of in her own language: it was either that, or no lessons at all. She was never at the top of the class, but never at the bottom either, and she always did her best. She had a squint, which affected both her appearance and her eyesight, and spoke with a slight stammer, but neither problem seems to have bothered her particularly. The teachers all liked her, and so did the other girls, because she was good-hearted, kind and helpful, and always ready to join in whatever fun was going. She had a quick temper, but never bore a grudge. When she finished primary education she was advised to enrol in the Domestic Science School, but she said she wanted to be a Sister.

The Infant Jesus Sisters were all Europeans, but an African congregation, the Sisters of the Holy Family (*Jamaa Takatifa*), was being developed at Bafwabaka. Girls who expressed interest in joining were known as "aspirants," and had to move to Bafwabaka and attend the secondary school there. First, Alphonsine had to work hard for a whole extra year to pass her exams. Then in January 1953, when the lorry to Bafwabaka was ready to start, she jumped on with the other girls, and by the time Julienne heard what had happened, the thirteen-year-old was well on her way. Later that year Amisi returned to Wamba with wife number two. He built a big house with room for both her and Julienne to live with him together, and Julienne agreed to give it a try, but she couldn't come to terms with living in a polygamous household. To Alphonsine's distress, her parents separated.

Novitiate

In 1956 she was officially accepted as a postulant, and a year later she became a novice. This involved being given her religious name, becoming Sr Marie Clementine, and being clothed for the first time in a white habit and veil. Alphonsine was delighted to see both her father and her mother present at the ceremony and - even more importantly

- that they managed to avoid creating a scene while they were there. Afterwards she told the novice mistress how happy she was, because now she belonged to Jesus Christ. During the novitiate she continued her studies, working towards her teaching certificate, and on 5th August 1959 she made her first, temporary, vows.

Sr Clementine took her new duties as a teacher very conscientiously. She also looked after the school's boarding facility, helped with the Legion of Mary and the Xaverians (a youth group the students were encouraged to join), and was on a rota for cooking meals in the convent. She was always willing to do more than her fair share of the work, and she was shocked to see that some of the Sisters tried to wriggle out of the harder jobs. She always enjoyed chatting with her friends, but she also enjoyed praying. When an Italian Verona Sister gave her a little statuette of Our Lady which glowed in the dark, she was thrilled and said she'd keep it with her always. Something that really upset her was unfairness within the community. *Jamaa Takatifa* drew recruits from different tribes and social sectors over quite a wide area, but most came from Stanleyville (Kisangani), the regional capital, and had grown up in families that were better-off and more westernised than Sr Clementine's. She was sure some of the Sisters in positions of authority were practising favouritism, and nothing she herself did seemed to be right in their eyes. But a wise Sister advised her to think of Jesus, who was mocked and ill-treated by those he'd come to save. Her face lit up: she'd been shown a way to cope with the situation, and use it as something to help her grow spiritually.

Her elder sisters were now married, but in the eyes of her mother, who'd never truly grasped the meaning of her religious vocation, she herself was still uncommitted. So one day Julienne arrived to see her daughter, and demanded that she leave the convent and return home to help her with the younger girls who were still at school. But Sr Clementine repeated the words of the Gospel: "Once the hand is laid on the plough, no one who looks back is fit for the kingdom of God." When the Infant Jesus Sisters began admitting African candidates, some of the Sisters arranged to transfer, but Sr Clementine stuck by her commitment to the *Jamaa Takatifa*. In 1962 she happily renewed her vows, kneeling in front of Mgr Joseph Wittebols, Bishop of Wamba.

Civil strife

The Congo had gained its independence two years previously, very abruptly, and with virtually no preparation; fighting broke out immediately, foreign business interests engineered a secession bid by the mineral-rich southern province of Katanga, and within three months Joseph Mobutu had staged a coup and made himself dictator. The prime minister, Lumumba, was murdered, and an attempt by his supporters to hold out in Stanleyville was defeated. However early in 1964 the Lumumbists in the north-east launched a fresh insurgency. The rebel fighters, who called themselves "Simbas" (lions), captured large numbers of foreigners - plantation owners, businessmen and missionaries - and held them hostage, then went on a killing spree, murdering hundreds of thousands of Congolese political opponents, government employees and traditional chiefs. But by late November the forces of retribution were closing in on them: Mobutu's National Army was advancing steadily into the north-east, and Belgian parachutists, dropped from American planes, captured the airport at Stanleyville.

On 29th November the Sisters at Bafwabaka were enjoying a festive lunch, belatedly celebrating Sr Clementine's name day (the Feast of St Clement, which had fallen a few days previously). Suddenly a lorry drove up, and Simba fighters began climbing in through the windows. The officer in charge, Justin Segbande, was known to the community. He announced that the Americans were approaching, so he'd come to rescue the Sisters and take them to Wamba; they must all pack their bags and be ready to leave as soon as possible. They were suspicious, but could see they weren't going to be given a choice. Like the others, Sr Clementine went to pack her bag. Then she found the chaplain, Fr Marcel Ebombo, and knelt for a blessing before climbing into the waiting lorry. The Sisters all sat down on the lorry bed, with soldiers standing round them.

As it drove off, their blood ran cold as they heard the Simbas singing: "Oh, the little Wives of the Fathers, where will they go tonight? Each one of us will have one for himself…" The superior, Mother Leontine Kasima, was told by some of the Simbas that they'd massacred the bishop and all the priests in Wamba. She refused to believe them, but it was true.

The journey continued until nightfall, then resumed the next day. Every so often the lorry stopped, and the Simbas went on the rampage, looting and boozing. Then they met up with a car full of high-ranking Simba officers. Colonel Pierre Olombe got out, and ordered that the Sisters' rosaries, crucifixes and holy medals be taken away. The soldiers searched them roughly to find and seize all the religious items, but they didn't find Sr Clementine's statuette which she'd hidden in her pocket. Olombe then redirected the lorry towards Isiro. It reached the outskirts towards evening and stopped at a house where the officers were just finishing their dinner, after which Olombe started ferrying the Sisters in batches to another location, the so-called "Blue House," about a kilometre away. But Colonel Gaston Ngalo wanted Sr Clementine to stay behind and become his "wife." The celibacy of Catholic religious and clergy was something the Simbas found inconceivable; they took it for granted that the Sisters slept with the priests, and couldn't understand why they refused the same favour to them. Mother Kasima was determined not to leave without Sr Clementine. Ngalo grew increasingly infuriated. He slapped Mother Kasima, then started hitting Sr Clementine when she told him to leave Mother Kasima alone. He tore off her veil, but she wouldn't give in.

The death of Sister Clementine

Just then Olombe returned to fetch them, because at the Blue House the other Sisters were refusing to eat until everyone had arrived. During the meal, the others urged Sr Clementine to eat something, but she had no appetite. She whispered, "I really believe I'm going to die tonight. Pray for me. To defend my virginity, I'm ready to die, but pray for me." Next Olombe, as he'd planned all along, tried to divide the Sisters up and send them to different rooms to sleep, but they insisted on all staying together. Eventually he grabbed Sr Clementine and another of the younger Sisters. They thought he was drunk, but according to his own later admission he was high on cannabis. Several times he forced the two Sisters to get into his car, but each time they opened the door at the other side and got out again. Incandescent with rage, he seized a rifle from a soldier and turned on Sr Clementine. "I forgive you," she said, "because you don't know what you are doing." The butt of the gun came down on her head, and she collapsed. Olombe began shouting that she was attacking him, and two of the soldiers came running; they weren't carrying guns, only spears and knives. "Stab her right in the heart!" screamed the Colonel. Standing one on either side, they stabbed her repeatedly. Then Olombe stepped forward, pulled out his revolver and shot her in the chest.

The Sisters carried Sr Clementine into the house. She seemed unconscious, but they could feel a faint heartbeat, and she died cradled in their arms. It was about 1am on 1st December. At daybreak the Simbas took her away and buried her with a lot of other corpses in a common grave. But in July 1965 a search was made for her remains, and she was identified by her injuries and by the statuette in the pocket of her habit. Colonel Olombe was arrested and condemned to death, but in exchange for offering his military services to Mobutu in suppressing yet another insurgency, his sentence was commuted to five years' imprisonment.

During a visit to Kisangani in 1980, Pope John Paul II met with Sr Clementine's parents. Julienne could hardly believe what was happening "I'm a poor woman and I've spoken to the Pope… Was it really me that gave birth to this saint?" During the beatification ceremony, in Kinshasa in 1985, the Pope repeated in the name of the whole Church her words of forgiveness for Pierre Olombe.

Blessed Clementine Anuarite, beloved daughter of Africa, faithful sister of all God's people, you were faithful unto death to your vow of chastity. Help us, by your example and intercession, to be constantly attentive to God and at the service of our neighbour, and to hold firm to our baptismal promises. Through Christ our Lord. Amen.

Further Reading

Material in English on African saints and blesseds is often not readily available, but the following resources may be of interest:

General:
Meinardus, Otto F A, *Coptic Saints and Pilgrimages* (2007)
O'Malley, Vincent J, *Saints of Africa* (2001)
http://www.saintannes.co.za/African%20Saints.htm

Bl Ghebre-Michael and St Justin de Jacobis:
O'Mahoney, Kevin, *The Ebullient Phoenix Vol 1* (1982)
http://famvin.org/wiki/Ghebre_Michael

St Josephine Bakhita:
Maynard, Jean, *Josephine Bakhita*: *A Survivor of Human Trafficking* (London, Catholic Truth Society, 2015)
Zanini, Roberto Italo (tr Andrew Matt), *Bakhita*: *From Slave to Saint* (2013)

Ugandan Martyrs:
Curley, Marie Paul FSP and Hill, Mary Lea FSP, *Saints Alive! The Gospel Witnessed* (2013) - entries on Sts Joseph Mukasa, Charles Lwanga, and Companions.
Faupel, John F, *African Holocaust* (1962)

94

http://www.ugandamartyrsshrine.org.ug
http://www.africamission-mafr.org/
uganda_martyrs12gb.htm

Bl Victoria Rasoamanarivo:
Curley, Marie Paul FSP and Hill, Mary Lea FSP,
Saints Alive! The Gospel Witnessed (2013) - entry on Bl
Victoria Rasoamanarivo.

Bl Raphael Rafiringa:
http://www.lasalle.org/en/who-are-we/lasallian-holiness/
br-raphael-louis-rafiringa

Bl Isidore Bakanja:
Maynard, Jean, Isidore Bakanja (London, Catholic Truth
Society, 2001)

Bl Daudi and Bl Jildo:
http://www.jido.org.uk

Bl Cyprian Michael Tansi:
Isichei, Elizabeth, *Entirely for God* (1989)
http://www.onitsha-archdiocese.org/index.php/k2/blessed-
cyprian-michael-tansi

Bl Clementine Anuarite:
http://anuarite.org (in French)